THOUGHTS IN SOLITUDE.

THOUGHTS IN SOLITUDE.

THOUGHTS IN SOLITUDE.

In Honorem Dei.

" Look unto Me, and be ye saved, for I am God !"—Isaiah xlv. 22.

" I am thy shield and thy exceeding great reward."—Gen. xv. 1.

CHELTENHAM :

PUBLISHED BY THOMAS SHIPTON.

LONDON: J. MASTERS.

MDCCCLIII.

LONDON :
PRINTED BY JOSEPH MASTERS AND CO.,
ALDERSGATE STREET.

PREFACE.

THE thoughts expressed in this volume were written indeed, *only* for those, to whom they are dedicated, and *some* addressed, with not the slightest intention of ever going beyond a manuscript. The kind persuasion and indulgent judgment of one dear to the writer, induced their appearing in this form, but not without much misgiving. We are jealous of what we most love, oh how far more should we be, lest with unhallowed hand, we mar the awful beauty of things pertaining unto GOD—and though, venturing in fear, near the solemn subject of the soul's "hidden life with CHRIST in GOD," which our Divine Redeemer purchased for us, with a mystery of woe !—a depth of agony !—on which our spirits ponder in awe and dismay; yet can we not withhold our living (GOD grant our dying) testimony to the "loving kindness of Him" whose praise is above all praise! whose glorious love to show forth—and whose gracious will to accomplish—is the only real joy, the only happiness worth living for, either on this side the grave, or in that eternity to which we are hastening.

May He with " His blessing" bless this little tribute of love, from one " not worthy of the least of all His mercies"—its covert be " the shadow of His wings"!

CONTENTS.

THOUGHTS IN SOLITUDE.

On the Love of God.

Is it not better lonely, and alone, to live,
If Thou, O LORD! the glory of Thy Spirit give,
That so, at last, we may not lonely die?
And oh! if Thine alone, the gracious eye!
That marks the faint spirit, and the failing heart!
Oh! could we from that tender watching part,
Or from that lov'd, and gentle thraldom start?
Ah, no! sweet is the love of those most dear,
Far brighter, than aught else life has to cheer;
Sweet are kind words, and gentle looks,
Nought else in grief, the lone heart brooks,
From those, in whom our yearning spirits seek a shrine
And give, alas! a worship meet, for things Divine!
But, oh! far dearer is that great Love,
Which bore e'en Thee! from heaven above,

Thy wanderers lost " to seek and save,"
And ransom from an eternal grave!
To love us with a love unknown,
Save by blest spirits, round Thy throne.
Sweet LORD! on Thee, the fondest heart may stay,
Nor fear that love will ever pass away.
To Thee! the passionate mind may bring,
(Nor lay in vain, beneath Thy shelt'ring wing)
Of tenderness, her richest treasure ;
The soul's bright off'ring without measure!
Then! when we meet Eternity's dread bound,
We shall not seek, nor look in vain around,
For those dear arms, so wont to guard, and bless,
So full of deep, undream'd of tenderness :
Thou wilt not fail us! ah! if sought in life,
Thy gentle love will soothe the parting strife,
Like infants sleeping near a parent's heart,
Wilt Thou not bid us in " Thy peace depart?"
Safe in Thine ark! in Love's eternal breast,
Into the fathomless hav'n of Thy rest!

On the Presence of God.

I SEE Thee still! that glorious Form, once wrung
    with agony!
That pitying eye of love! for evermore is drawing
    me!
I see Thee, mid the hum of men,
By the soft still waters, and when
No eye, or heart is near, I see Thee still!
Thine angel is withholding me from ill.
But, oh! in solitude, " Thy Spirit strives,"
Resistless still, Thy claim of love revives,
And then, my silent spirit looks on high,
And feels no more alone, for Thou art nigh!
Ah! holy is that hour! too pure for such as me,
That solemn antecedent of eternity.
Yes, awful 'tis to feel Thee near;
Uphold us, in that hour most dear.
Such joy our failing spirits could not bear,
Nor to behold " that glory," might they dare,
Did not the soul, in fear, in mystery, feel
What Thou alone, so brightly canst reveal!

I see Thee still! when darkness nears,
While gather o'er the spirit fears
Of Thy dread sanctity!   Ah! then, there shines
A glory, not of this world, that divines
Things shown us, as in a vision of sweet hope,
That we might strengthen'd be, with the rude world
   to cope ;
But when its fatal hopes are o'er,
And we near the eternal shore,
Oh let me see Thee still! in that dark hour
Enshroud me in Thine Atoning Power!
Let no dread thoughts my failing spirit shake,
When falling in that sleep, whence none shall wake!
Ah! to see THEE then! when our life itself shall fail,
And mortal hope, oh what save Thy great love avail?
Oh joy! to which no thought, no dream of hope e'er
   soared
In our dying hearts, to feel THEE, everlasting LORD!

On Prayer.

OH priceless gift! too little felt, immeasurably dear!
For 'tis with CHRIST, our Love Divine, to seek com-
    munion near;—
'Twould seem a foretaste of the skies,
Where tears fall not from mortal eyes.
And such indeed, to those is given
Who love Him best, on this side heaven,
Oh bright! for ever blessed joy—mysterious boon,
The secret Thine to tell, how sweetly, and how soon
Man shall on earth, his SAVIOUR find in prayer!
Though wandering still, a lonely outcast there.
Through His sweet sacrifice, how sorely wrought!
He! who from highest heav'n our cold hearts sought.
By it; the yearning spirit soars,
E'en to the everlasting doors;
Ah then, she finds her joyful wings,
To venture near the King of Kings!
At His great throne, to pour our heart's best tears,
Though striving still, 'tween chasten'd hopes and
    fears.

Then, then indeed, CHRIST's pledge is given,
For to be with Him, alone is heav'n!
Oh! weak all words to tell the glorious tale,
At which the sav'd, the holiest saint grows pale,
Behold the Lamb! GOD's gift divine!
In spirit touch Him! call Him thine!
In prayer, though voiceless, hold Him fast,
Until He bless thee: then at last,
Thine heart shall feel, thine eye shall see,
And "less than dross, count all but He!"
'Tis then, the chain'd tongue shall cry aloud,
Loosëd from fear's dark despairing cloud;
The soul, unshackled from sin's weary clod,
Shall lovingly "stretch forth her hands to GOD!"
And ask no sweeter boon, until her latest breath,
Save to be His alone! bright hope in life and death!
He will not spurn the spirit's fears,
Nor turn from her unbidden tears,
While to His awful throne she nears.

On those taken away from us.

Oh! stay them not, their course is run,
The bright, the blessed crown is won!
They've seen the Form Benign,
They've heard the Voice Divine!
" My love, My fair one, come away"—
Detain them not, nor ask their stay.
From henceforth! their hearts are thrilling
With the joy that is fulfilling,
To see that Face of Love
Shine brightly from above :
To hear that Voice so dear,
Their longing spirits cheer,
With words divine, of sweetest stay :—
" Arise! My fair one! come away!"
Behold now, the rain is past,
The withering, wintry blast
Of death, and sin, and woe!
The blight on all below.
But now, " the flowers appear,"
And the birds with songs so clear.

Oh the hills of light afar,
Where is peace!—sin cannot mar :
Where life is ceaseless love
And glory from above.
Lo! "the Great Shepherd" evermore is near
Unto the "little flock" He bought so dear!
In whose arms there is repose.
Nor e'er shall the curtains close,
Of that dawn of endless light,
And of Goodness Infinite!
Yea, "now the dawn has broken,
    The shadows disappear:"
The blessed sounds there spoken,
    Fall on no earthly ear.
Oh Thou! the brightness Infinite! all gracious and
    divine;
Ah, whisper to my fainting heart, " Thou art Mine,
    for ever Mine !"

On our Lord's Presence in Death.

AND Thou! wilt make it sweet to die;
Sweeter than angel's ministry;
For, in that hour, Thou LORD! wilt come to me,
And take my happy spirit unto Thee!
Oh, sleep of glory! in Thy bosom hid,
Thy long lost child of earth, so fondly chid,
Through many tears, yet gently drawn
From earthly love, to that bright morn.
Ah! Thou in glory "hast gone up on high"
To be with Thy redeemëd, still more nigh!
On "mansions long prepar'd," oh! shed Thy light,
That we may live for ever in Thy sight.
That heav'n was bought with tears of blood!
With agony's o'erwhelming flood!
Oh LORD! my GOD! oh what are we?
The purchase of that agony!
Yet come, complete Thy work of love,
Send down Thine angels from above;
"The FATHER" waits Thy flock to see,
For whom He gave,—He gave e'en Thee!

That through Eternity's exhaustless span,
No name, save Thine alone! might sound from man.
Come, LORD! from death Thou tak'st the pain,
" To die and to depart is gain;"
Ah! come! for if the spirit sees Thy face,
Vision of GOD! oh, what shall it efface?
The soul, transformed by Thee, for joy shall bow her
    head,
Too blessed to be numbered with the holy dead!

On Depression.

THERE is a time when the soul weeps! sad and lone,
And through her anguished cells, roam thoughts,
    whose tone,
Would clothe her in sin, till o'er our bosom's night
Thy Spirit breathes! hiding all evil from our sight:—
Oh, in that dark, and dangerous hour,
Still guide us to Thy shelt'ring bower,—
And draw us to those living wells,
Where Thine Eternal Goodness dwells!
'Tis when " Thou hid'st Thy face," our spirits fail,
Forgetting then, Thy love doth still prevail,
Through that deep woe, to make us strive to look
    above,
And long to wake in the full sunshine of Thy Love!
Ah then it is, that Thy bright presence blooms,
Like flowerets blossoming mid the tombs;
Then 'tis, Thy Spirit brings across the mind,
Sweet yearnings! strange, as light is, to the blind!
'Tis then, we feel that Thou art there,
And still vouchsaf'st our griefs to share!

While the deep chasten'd spirit turns to Thee!
To Thy lone grief! to "Thy dread agony!"
Ah then! our dear Redeemer's tears,
Fall on the heart, and blot out years
Of sin and woe!—nor could we wish the strife away,
That bid the light, the glory, of Thy presence stay.
Yes! dear that weary grief! how keen soe'er!
The germ of Immortality is there!
Oh! in that hour, when none are nigh,
Save the bright witnesses on high,
Send down Thy pitying angel, LORD,
From Thy dread presence, oh most Ador'd!
And bid him pass his snowy wing
O'er our dull hearts' sad suffering;
And heal the ravages of woe
That strangely wound us here below!—
Then from that darkness, the soul shall light
Upon a vision of fair sight,
As though 'twere given us to see,
The glories of Eternity!

On Holy Scripture.

THERE is a blessing in Thy words divine,
Where " GOD's great glory" doth for ever shine!
So full of beauty, and of promise sure,
Cheering the wearied spirit to endure :—
Oh happy ones! whose mine of gold Thou only
  art,
Blessed indeed! who in the book of life have part—
Who seek and search with loving heart—who fondly
  pray,
Till on " Thy mighty truth," Thou dost their spirits
  stay!
Ah! there Thou reveal'st things too bright
For human thought, for mortal sight;
Those thrilling hopes that round the spirit stray,
As onward still, Thine angel leads the way.
Oh! cause our eyes to see, our hearts to feel,
" That hope of glory!" and to us reveal
Thyself! yea, realize Thy love, so near,
For sinful man, alas! 'twould seem too dear!

Lost creature of the dust! whom Thou hast deigned
   to raise,
That he might find no joy so precious, as Thy
   praise.
Sweetness ineffable! whose gracious love,
Shining, in pity endless, from above,
Can make the wilderness to bloom,
And gather life, from out the tomb!
Show us Thy secrets in Thy true word!
By the world that knows Thee not, unheard.
In the bright folds of Thine own presence hide us—
   Thy Spirit breathe
Upon Thine own, too dearly loved!—around their
   hearts, oh wreathe
Hopes, that lead the soul to that calm sweet night,
Whose dawn shall be in " everlasting light!"
The hour shall come, when other knowledge shall
   avail us not,
When the lost soul shall turn in horror from her
   world-won lot;
But those who lean upon the cross—the anchor of all
   hope—
Oh what wisdom shall be theirs! with which earth
   may never cope.
They know that by that cross,
For which the world is loss,

Heaven's portals are lifted high,
For " His redeemed to pass by;"—
" There shall they know, as they are known,"
There shall God claim them, for His own.
But here, " as in a glass we see,"
That hidden Holy Mystery!
The charter of their hope—the record of His love—
   how dear they hold,
Which shall to them, each day, some new delight,
   some dearer hope unfold!
Oh then mourn we not! as those who have no token,
For though " the spirits fail," the tried hearts be
   broken,
They shall yet " the robe of His great beauty" wear;
The likeness of uncreated glory bear!
And though the heart be failing,
Shall in His love prevailing,
Meet, where joy is not, as a fading dream,
As it will here below too often seem,
But a bright ray of the Eternal beam!

On Forgetfulness of God.

Oh no! it is not death, " to fall asleep in Him!"
Before whom bow the cherubim and seraphim;
To leave the memory of our tears below,
" Following the LAMB OF GOD where'er He go!"
To feel the angel's arms around us cast!
Or e'er that lonely valley shall be past.
Ah! better so to die! than feel,
The living death of sin reveal
Forgetfulness of THEE, O GOD! Darkness, how
  deep!
That cold and still, that undisturb'd, and deathly
  sleep!
For the dull heart Thy goodness spurns,
And from Thy dear love ever turns:
From joys, on which the angels gaze,
In sad and wondering amaze—
Oh! is it thus? till we provoke Thee to forsake,
From us to " hide Thy face!" the spirit's darkness
  make,

While evil of our better thought gets mastery. \
Yes, so it is, we love Thee not ! nor think of Thee ; \
Who, by Thine own ! Thy wondrous off'ring set
   us free!

And yet for us, " that glorious Head" in death did
   bow!

And Thy prevailing efficacy is o'er us now!

At GOD's right hand, Thou reign'st! Oh righteous
   Judge of all!

And stayest the hand uprais'd ! on Thy redeemed to
   fall.

Thine are we! Thine alone, Thine evermore,

In life and death! darkness and trial sore.

Almighty Justifier! " Thy little flock behold,"

"Thine everlasting arms" around us, oh! sweetly fold;

Guide safely, through earth's deep treachery and guile

To the ineffable sunshine of Thy smile!

On the Gifts of God.

FROM out Thy sacred treasury above,
Give! "without measure give!" to me Thy love;
That sweetest boon the soul can crave,
In all Thy ceaseless goodness gave,
That precious love! which Thou hast giv'n to all,
Through mighty sorrows, that on the spirit call
In awful warning!   But power, that love to feel,
Is Thine alone to give: to us "Thyself reveal!"
Yea, happy are they that seek Thee! more blessed
    still,
Who steadfast set, to do, and suffer all Thy will,
Shall find Thee! the treasure of the soul is there,
That precious secret which no heart can share.
To whom alone, the "priceless pearl" is freely given,
"That favour, that better is than life," that love our
    heav'n!
There is no hope that earth doth bring,
Can soothe the spirit's suffering—
No joy is there, like this, the tongue can tell,
Springing from the glad heart's deep hidden cell—

For that, is the voiceless yearning
Of the soul in sorrow turning,
To that well of quenchless joy
Which time shall ne'er destroy!
When immortality is dawning
Upon the spirit's deathless morning,
And Thy lov'd ones, too deeply blest,
Shall find a foretaste of Thy Rest!

Oh crown us not with earthly gifts, far from Thy
    love's thrall,

While the deep thirstings of our immortal nature
    call

On THEE! Eternal GOD! and only THEE!
Who art the Heaven of Eternity!

On the Holy Communion.

THERE! if any where, Thou deignest to wait,
Still bending, from the chamber of Thy state,
Thy tender arms held forth unto Thy lost ones! to
    revive
" The hearts that fail," and for them still, with death
    and darkness strive.
Oh good and gracious GOD! and can it be?
That we should still refuse to come to Thee!
Forbid it, LORD! by Thy dread offering! by that last
    night,
Which darkly usher'd in the morn of our undying
    light,
By the dear thoughts of Thine eternal love, so true,
(Though we from day to day Thine agony renew!)
By that Thy love! which stay'd not on Thy coming
    strife of woe,
But on us! to whom Thou would'st " seal its glory"
    here below,

Oh deathless—awful words! "In remembrance of
  Me,"

"This do"—until I come My death shall set forth
  be!

Ah! when Thou bidd'st Thy servant to Thyself draw
  nigh,

Still, be the angel of Thy loved presence nigh,

That so, my ransom'd spirit justified, and free,

Through that Thine own, too precious death, may
  pass to Thee!

On Preparation for the Holy Communion.

MINE hallow'd preparation, O LORD, my GOD! art
    Thou!
Thy robe of beauty give, oh give, and heal my spirit
    now!
" The tree of life," in Paradise, is freely offered here
In that oblation all divine! so awful and so dear.
And " blessed are the mourners;" yea, and blest the
    broken heart,
Who in the " Holy Eucharist" most surely have their
    part.
Ah! could we see the angel eyes, that watch o'er us
    from on high,
We should not need to ask again, if the LORD OF
    LIFE is nigh;
Whose tender arms are round us, by whom the
    worlds were made,
Whose form Divine is near us,—Who on the cross
    was laid !
The spell of sin is brok'n, the gate of hell o'erthrown,
While wakes within the heart, a sorrow, not yet known.

" We look on Him we pierc'd!" so glorious, and so
 dread!

On Him! who for our sakes, was numbered with the
 dead.

" The altogether lovely!"—to love Him!—gift too
 dear,

Dawning on the heart forgiv'n! that He alone can
 cheer.

For such, life hath no solitude! nor death the sting of
 pain;

To them, it is the sun-lit gate of everlasting gain!

To see Him, who thus loved them, e'en to the gate of
 death,

Whose " pierc'd hands" shall cover them! to their
 latest dying breath!

On Past Illness.

It was Thy precious love! Thy pleading pow'r,
Thy servant ransomed from that dreadful hour,
From delirium's deadly grasp—
From dreary phantoms of the past—
To restore Thy lost one, to "Thy FATHER's love,"
And fit her for Thy radiant home above!
That still mid life, and grief's long thoughtful day,
Her soul might "rest in hope!" nor turn away,
That by Thy sweet pity, she might e'er
Thy glorious name repentant bear,
And Thy celestial "breastplate" wear.
Ah! by that Thy love, so dear, so true,
Which from death's dark gate my soul withdrew!
Withdraw not Thou, Thyself, my GOD! "Thy face
    hide not from me:"
Oh! then life were too desolate—no home where I
    could flee!
Cast not Thy ransomed child away,
To whom, Thou art the dearest stay.

Who, that has known Thy love's great boon!
Without it, but must wither soon?
Who, that has felt that hope so fair,
Could deem thus sad, ought other care
As the dread loss of Thee, dearer than the miser's
    gold,
More precious far, than all the treasure earth can
    hold?
Give me Thyself, my SAVIOUR dear!
Painless is sorrow, if Thou art near.
Without Thee, life is not; it is but death!
Oh darker far—than that which stills our breath!
Then on me "cause Thy face to shine,"
A joy for man, all too Divine!
Thine, this to give, Incarnate LORD!
Through Whom alone, the gift is pour'd,
That when our gladdened hearts within us burn,
Ah then we might, with a spirit's eye, discern
A foretaste of that land of light,
Where Thou alone mak'st all things bright!
Oh! who but Thee? the soul's immortal aim,
Her deathless trust from Thy sweet Spirit came!
That is the mystery of Thy thrilling love;
Which makes us look, and long, for heaven above,
Those sights to see, those sounds to hear,
Which day by day we feel so near!

D

Those joys to taste by man unknown,
By Thine exhaustless goodness shown!
Oh gracious LORD! benign and true,
Ah! who shall give Thee worship due?
How blest are they, to whom Thou art most dear,
Blessed is the spirit that Thou shalt cheer!
Blessed are they to whom Thou com'st in pow'r,
Unearthly warnings of the solemn hour!

On Gentleness.

THE Spirit's meaning in that tender word, is hid in.
　　one unseen,
Who, for us, stood alone, in the dread pass! GOD's
　　wrath, man's guilt between.
In us, that bright thing is not! although we call it so,
Unless from Him 'tis giv'n us, to show-forth here
　　below.
In Him 'twas seen with bleeding brow and unrepining
　　love!
On whom the Spirit rests alone! in form as of a
　　Dove.
Oh that no will but His were ours,
'Mid life's sad, and darkened hours!
No other guide be given
To light us into heaven!
Call it not gentleness; the world's bland tone,
Ah! be not this, the law our spirits own!
Oh! false unto our Great Eternal King!
That worldly science, not from Him, we bring.

His awful Brow of Glory, but wore the crown of
    thorn!

Yea, "the High, the Holy One," was bowed down
    with scorn!

Ah! seek it there! where GOD's own "brightness"
    lay,

While darkness wrapt that sacred Form from day!

Oh! never was archangel's worship so intense as
    then,

When still for us, His gentle spirit bore the scorn of
    men!

When on the dreary cross, "GOD's well Beloved" had
    lain!

Perhaps in heaven were tears, ne'er to be shed again.

What tears of love! when to His FATHER's care He
    did resign His breath,

Almighty offering! breaking in twain the iron bonds
    of death!

Oh! wise of this world, behold GOD's wisdom there,

That in that precious Thing thou too may'st share,

Alas! "the princes of this world knew it not!"

Blinded by the false wisdom of their lot;

Oh that they had known it! nor brought the crime

Of His too Precious Blood! His Death sublime!

Upon that guilty land He trod,

And "crucified the LORD their GOD!"

But oh! not only they, we too
Forsake Thee! crucify anew!
Redeemer! LORD! could we but feel Thee nigh,
So clasp Thy pierced feet, and daily die!

On Sorrow.

It is not time, oh! what is it, that blots out the hope
    of years,
Leaving us, of those fond dreams of joy, no vestige
    save our tears ?
The broken heart knows what it is, it need not here
    be told,
All earthly hopes are vanity, now, as in time of old !
Oh! tell us not of joys to come, on earth it may
    not be,
Until the heir of sorrow is from sin for ever free !
Our deathless spirits pine alone,
Till we " our FATHER's" presence own !
Of joy's full measure we can little know,
Exiled—in a vale of tears below!
But Feet Divine this earth too meekly trod,
To garner in the forfeit souls to GOD !
Their solace and their refuge He alone !
Who turneth into peace our hearts of stone,
When all that we here, have loved so well,
All that we trusted to, too dear to tell !

When all shall fail, and shall the hearts cast away ⎫
To break as they will, in that sorrowing day, ⎬
Without hope or support of this world's false stay; ⎭
'Tis then that love unchang'd enfolds the soul,
With boundless hope! with joy beyond control!
Ah then, doth His Spirit on the sick heart light,
Soft'ning to day the dreariest dreams of night:
But we still turning from that peaceful ray,
Will still seek homes on earth, in hearts of clay,
And for our too fond affections find a tomb!
Oh! "Thou the morning star!" Ah! shine on that
   deep gloom,
Our soul's true light, our heart's sole stay,
Spare us! nor cast us quite away!
When sorrow's depths, and grief and wrong,
Shall throw their darkling shade along
Our path,—ah then stretch forth Thine arms of love,
Draw us unto Thy tearless home above:
Oh! o'er us cast Thy wings of peace,
And bid the strife of sorrow cease!

On my Burial.

Oh lay me in the hallowed ground—my long'd for
  sleep of joy!
Which no pow'r of sin, or sorrow, shall e'er trouble
  or destroy.
There, peace shall be eternal! the spirit is at rest;
The soul's desire is granted! to be of God possess'd!
I would not grieve the much prized hearts that I
  have lov'd so well;
I would not cause their tears to flow, nor their hearts
  with grief to swell.
But, I would pray each dear one, by the love of long
  past years,
To seek "the only refuge" now, from everlasting
  tears!
As though my spirit, (from her promis'd rest in God,)
Would warn them of the path, that faithless ones
  have trod.
Oh! could our eyes be open'd, as they shall one day be,
No need were there to urge this most dread and so-
  lemn plea,

"Flee from the wrath to come!" make Him thy
  portion now,
Who wore the rending crown on "His Incarnate
  brow!"
Ah! language fails, the secret of that joy to tell,
Seek it then, oh seek, at the everliving well!
The well of living waters! the deep fount of "Holy
  Blood!"
What tears, what sighs, shall rise to Him like one
  vast water flood.
One only hand has right those tears to wipe
  away!
It is the Pierced One! our never failing stay!
Oh! "seek Him while He may be found," ah, "call
  while He is near,"
The time shall be, when He, our GOD, shall cease to
  lend an ear!
And when the earth shall press my breast, with many
  hopes gone by,
Telling again the solemn tale of life's futility;
Oh! had I then an angel's tongue, I would from its
  lustre borrow,
And cry with tears of anguished love, Oh, wait not
  for the morrow!
"This the day of salvation is! The accepted time is
  now!"

Oh think! if it pass unheeded by, what remorse, thine
    heart shall bow!
Dark and subtle is the foe, that seeks thy spirit's fall!
Entangling thy careless thoughts in his most deadly
    thrall.
Oh! GOD forbid! that curse should light upon thy
    brow :—
The thrilling voice still whispers "Come unto Me
    now!"
Seek but of Him the knowledge; make sure that He
    is thine:
"All is but loss, to win Him," brightness of joy
    divine!
Oh hasten then to cast thy soul on His most loving
    breast,
Who bought for thee, with tears of blood, that fore-
    taste of His rest!

On Loneliness.

Ah! deem it not so sad to be alone,
Though our fairest joys are from love's dear tone,
But brighter with blessing is that still lone hour,
When the Love Divine has a mightier pow'r!
For there are no tears so deep, that GOD cannot heal,
When to the spirit He deigns His love to reveal.
Ah! sweeter in His arms to lie,
And learn that sacred mystery,
Than the gladdening tide of this world's love,
For which we forfeit the glory above!
Oh! broken hearts! for whom He died!
Who have not yet that dear love tried!
All that our fond youth's dreams can know,
All that is felt of bliss below,
However bright, untold, or dear,
Of happiness, the heart can cheer,
Is darkness—to that sweet thrilling voice!
Without which, Heaven could not rejoice!
That is the joy of death, when nearer our LORD shall be,
O'ershadowing us, " that blessed FORM OF DEITY!"

On His Bosom Divine to fall asleep,
And wake where the angels their sabbath keep.
Ah, bright is that goal of this life's tears !
Worthy the suff'rings of countless years.
Then weep not, when tearful eyes shall close
To sin and sorrow, and all earth's woes :—
Call not the spirit from her awful rest,
From the depths of joy in her SAVIOUR's breast!
" Ye know not what ye do!"   Oh turn !
And seek in solitude to learn,
How GOD from death can take the sting,
And to the sainted spirit bring
The victory!   For this He died, the all ador'd,
In love's deep agony, to His FATHER poured,
The precious off'ring that alone could save,
That Death Divine that overcame the grave !
Ah! who shall tell what love, in that hour of awe,
Shall from death its terrors and its sting withdraw !
The spirits believing shall never die, nor find
That last woe which the false and the faithless shall
    bind,
In life !   They found death from their dear LORD
    parted,
In the lonely path of the broken-hearted;
But their tears have ceased ! and none can sever,
The enfolding love, that is theirs for ever !

To .. ..

In youth—that morning dream! how beautiful and
    fair,
Which, hearts like thine—would make more truth,
    more brightness wear,
Then Hope, and Love—ah! strong are ye, life's ills
    to greet,
Nor would reject, (in your fond strength) that off'ring
    meet,
Thus,—the cold, far world was nought to me,
While wandering there, alone with thee!
And when in after years,
Mid smiles, and hopes, and tears,
The memory of that tender love,
(Like a bright messenger from above,)
Would softly rest upon my spirit's sorrow,
To gather hope, and from its brightness borrow,
Then, in all griefs, would thy dear smile,
From mournful thoughts my spirit wile,
And to sweet hopes my heart beguile!

E

Yes, I have lov'd thee well! and lov'd thee then
As few, perchance, may ever love again.
Ah! were I righteous, for thee, I fain would pray,
That light and life divine—might lead thee on thy
    way,
Yet One there is, who pleadeth with Almighty love,
" The brightness of His FATHER's glory," throned
    above!
No boon is there of earth could meet my love for
    thee,
For I would ask a glorious immortality!
Of such full joy, as for GOD's own too well belov'd
    is meet,
Where the undying spirit rests at her Redeemer's
    feet.
Oh, brightly borne upon the waves of life's dark
    troubled sea,
Unto the shoreless ocean of eternity!
There may we meet, mine own dear love,
In GOD's bright Paradise above!
There! there, in peace unbroken,
May those great words be spoken—
" Where is thy sting? oh death! thy victory where?
    oh grave!"
" The ransom His!" " most mighty," from Death
    and Hell to save!

On Love.

Most blessed are they to whom 'tis given,
To know no stay but God! no hope but heav'n!
We call them lonely!—oh! did they, could they
    know,
How peaceful is the boon, allotted them below!
They would not look, with longing eyes around,
On those in earthly ties so strongly bound!
Alas! what, if beneath, those flow'rs of love,
(Which seem to hide the mysteries above,)
God's dread and solemn judgments lie!
The love betray'd!—the hopes that die—
While hearts unclaim'd are call'd away! or e'er too
    late,
Before their loving spirits have grown desolate.
Ah! better not to know its sad and fearful power,
For if 'tis blighted, on the heart 'twill pour a shower
Of woe unknown!—too sad, too bitter still,
E'en for this darkling world of wrong and ill!
Like a mighty tempest, crushing the sweet flow'rs,
That seemed to bloom alone for heavenly bow'rs,

Breaking the fond true heart on which it falls,
Or withering it with grief, that more appals!
Ah! such is earthly love!—a thing so bright,
That dearest hopes might blossom in its light,
Till we wake from those sweet, fond thoughts of bliss,
For 'tis but a dream, in a world like this!
Oh! sad is that waking!—and dark is that hour,
To find time, and change, on such love hath power!
And yet, there is a changeless love on earth—
From out the skies it took its kindly birth—
Its perfect beauty comes across the mind,
As a veil cast o'er sorrows left behind!
Like dew drops, sent from out the heav'ns above,
To show our fallen souls, the truth of Love!
That we might bring the chasten'd heart,
Which lies all stricken, and apart!
And lay it gently 'neath the wing,
Of that dear Love's fond covering!
That love is Thine alone! sweet LORD of life!
Who meekly sufferedst earth's dark, drear strife!
Holy! Immortal One! Who diedst to bind,
Our restless spirits round the Eternal Mind!

On Heaven.

DREAM of Heaven! foretaste of a brighter thing,
Oh! o'er our wearied spirits, promise bring!
Of still dearer hopes to come!—where Thou, O LORD!
   dost hide,
Thy goodness! and Thy beauty! oh! evermore abide
With Thine own redeemed of earth—
Till Thou shalt seal their second birth,
There, in the star-pav'd land,
Where the bright angels stand!
Upon the waveless shore,
When time shall be no more!
'Tis there alone the living waters flow,
Where e'en the broken heart forgets her woe—
It is " the tree of life" there stands,
Stretching afar her " healing" hands—
Ah! then, at last, we shall behold that Face Divine!
Vision of unearthly glory! Form Benign!
That, is the joy, " man's heart cannot conceive"!
Upon his transform'd spirit to receive,

That likeness fair! Divinely Fair!

"Breastplate" of all that enter there,

"To drink of the Vine" at GOD's right hand,

And in "His righteousness" to stand,

To wake in life eternal!—which so many cast away.

Won by His sorrows infinite! what love shall e'er
    repay?

Ah yes! that heav'n is prepared,

For those indeed that love Thee! shar'd

By them alone—Blessed Hope! oh! passing glorious,

"In the Beloved One!" to be found victorious.

They are "the pure in heart!"—made such indeed by
    Thee!

Sole Mysterious Author of all Purity!

And Thou wilt plant them in Thy sweetest home
    of love,

Thy beautiful, Thine endless Paradise above!

On Death.

Ah! when at last the midnight call I hear,
Which bids me unto life! to God! draw near,
When the strife of life is o'er,
And " the Judge is at the door"!
When the dread, the solemn angel stands!
With pitying eye, and outstretch'd hands!
Call it not death! we may not weep, nor grieve to
    die,
If " Thou, the Resurrection and the life" be nigh!
Oh! blest and bright! the spirit's sweet repose,
Who 'neath Thy cross have garner'd all their woes!
No visions scare!—no fearful thoughts molest,
While angels wait, to bear them to their rest.
They shall not strive, nor ever fail,
For " not by strength, shall they prevail"!
Ah!—is it not gain to die? " far better" to be with
    Thee!
While Thou art still the light! the life of our
    eternity!

Our dear ones, in Thine arms to leave in peace,
And pass away !—where time and shadows cease !—
Oh! sweetest of all joys, it is, to do Thy will!
But evermore to be with Thee—is dearer still!
To feel that Thou wilt " ne'er forsake" our lov'd
    ones left below,
But to them give the sacred boon—Thy glorious love
    to know !
In Thy bright arms, for ever them uphold !
And soon, and safely, bring them to Thy fold—
In that last awful hour, alone " I look to Thee !"⎫
In Thine Atoning Love—oh! set my spirit free, ⎬
Jesus! Redeemer! Lord Most High! remember me!⎭

To E . . . . .

May'st thou but live to do His will!
Through grief and trial, wrong and ill,
His will! " who trod the winepress of God's wrath,"
   for thee!
In patient love—Divine, and awful sanctity!
So shall thy spirit God's great Glory see,
And the bright angels shall have charge of thee!
Oh! if in thy young manhood's prime,
Thou would'st give heed before the time
Shall come to thee, that comes to all!
Nor vainly let God's Spirit call,
In youth,—upon thine heart; oh! believe!
Lest that subtle spirit thee deceive,
And rob thee of both worlds! for if heaven is won;
   be sure
Earth too is thine! nor pang hath it too heavy to
   endure!
Think then! oh think Who 'twas thy spirit gave,
He,—who, on earth's cold breast, but sought a
   grave,

To save thee from the curse of sin's unrest,
To win thy deathless soul into His breast!
That priceless, untold joy be thine!
Oh! slight it not—while yet there's time,
Turn not again to this world's hollow smile,
While angels wait, aye, watch for thee, the while.
Who shall assure thee of to-morrow's sun?
Ah! who shall tell thee when thy race is run?
That secret is with " Him who once His Glory" left,
And of heaven's full joy His gentle spirit reft
For thee!—His Hand Divine upholds thee still,
Then to His Love resign thy steadfast will!
Oh! forfeit not that glorious dower,
Nor covet thou the worldling's power!
But turn!—and evermore that Mighty Sufferer be-
   hold!"
" Fight the good fight of faith! and on eternal life
   lay hold!"
Ah! yet at GOD's right hand!—still, still " He
   pleads,"
For thee, and thine, for ever intercedes!
In that most sweet, that ever blessed hope,
With sin and wrong!—GOD give thee strength to
   cope!
And on thine happy path to endless day,
Grieve not, nor blame the sorrows of the way!

It is God's Spirit leads, whate'er betide.

Ah! only watch! and feel Him by thy side!

"His angel calls"! oh seek, nor turn away,

Lest darkness wrap thee from eternal day!

He will not fail thee! repentant cast thy soul on
  Him.

"The crucified!"—the worship of the seraphim!

Then, when thy lonely journey shall be made,

And what was young, and bright, and fair, shall fade,

He! that bought thee His for ever,

Will not from His promise sever!

Nor shalt thou fear, or sigh,

As the angel passes by!

To bear thee on his wings of light,

To the Throne of uncreated Might!

Thy trusting spirit shall not weep,

When falling in death's dreamless sleep!

For safe in the "everlasting arms"!

For ever freed from all alarms!—

'Tis God that calls thee into heaven to see,

The joys "thy Saviour" has prepar'd for thee!

On Faith.

It is a sure belief, in His Great " Word" !
Which God Himself must give ! where not unheard,
His Spirit rests indeed !   For once in this dark
    world was seen,
" One ! like unto the sons of men"! but oh! so calm !
    serene !
" In whom the fulness of the Godhead dwelt!"
While near that Awful Glory, wise men knelt,
" God's gift of love unspeakable" to receive !
And these, ah! these, the world no more, hath pow'r
    to deceive.
" Within the veil, their anchor they have cast,"
Doubt's dreary shadows are for ever past !
They have not seen Him, and yet " they love,"
Begun beneath, and perfected above !
The light of God shines full upon the " narrow road,"
Guiding in peace unknown ! unto His lov'd abode,
Henceforth, no hopes of earth shall dazzle with
    strange light,

Ere long, their eyes shall look upon a fairer sight,

"All things are theirs!" for they are His, and from
His love,

Oh! who shall part them—from "that name? all
names above!"

Words have no strength, nor voice hath pow'r,

To tell the brightness of that hour,

When "He was found of them." "Let not their
hearts be troubled:" how near

He is—they know not; for, He may seem as though
He did not hear!

Unto these broken spirits shall He not reveal,

What from the world lies hid? His dear ones surely
heal!—

Yes! fondly, firmly, let them cleave unto His love!
and He,

The Great, the Glorious Fruition of their faith,
shall be!

On Holiness.

Sweet and dread emblem of God's Purity! Ah! well,
Yet hidden in thy solemn beauty, dost thou dwell,
Deep in the lone, the chasten'd heart,
Where God has been! and is! Thou art
But the still echo of "His Spirit's voice"!
That in that blessedness we might rejoice,
And "follow on to know Him"! haply find
The glorious traces of that mighty mind,
And round our hearts His Love Eternal bind.
The very air is full of voices sweet! of joys so near,
Yea! and of warnings sad, and solemn, that we will
   not hear!
Is not "the Holy Spirit" nigh?
God's own Great Gift to prove us by!
Purchased by Him who made this world so fair,
And died!—that sinlessly we might walk there!
Ah! there is nought on earth so fair as Thee!
Martyr sublime! our Immortality!
'Tis Thy great love that brightens life's sad flowers,
Giving them the bloom of heavenly bowers.

Yes, awful in Thine Holiness art Thou!

Cause us to seek "that glorious gift" e'en now,

Without which, none shall see Thy Face! O LORD!
  my GOD!

That ere our tearful hearts shall sleep 'neath earth's
  cold sod,

Thou'lt clothe us in "Thy mantle bright,"

Thy garment dread of spotless white!

And bring us home, where hopes eternal are! where
  sorrows cease!

And where Thine own too dearly won—shall rest with
  Thee in peace!

On Riches.

VAINLY Thou givest earthly treasure,
Increasing riches without measure!
Unless Thy smile, O LORD, turn all to gold!
That sweetest alchymy of hope untold!—
Where is Thy secret hid? Thy priceless "Peace,"
That unknown joy, where all repinings cease!
Surely, it is vouchsafed e'en here below,
To holy hearts and true, though faint and slow,
The treasure of the soul art Thou! the hope of every
 day,
The glorious host of heav'n afar! could ask no dearer
 stay.
The riches of the universe, are darkness unto Thee!
Who art "The Brightness"! yea, the bliss of our
 eternity!
We toil with aching heart and brow,
The secret here of joy to know—
That secret so deep! some, alas! cannot find;
And yet 'tis given to the lowliest mind!

Yes! there are riches of measureless span,
Neither hid nor withheld from sinful man;
But we steal on in darkness, nor look on high,
To the sweet goal of our endless destiny!
Poor mourners! oh seek then, "to know the LORD!"
Nor one look cast back on the miser's hoard.
Mortal heart could not bear such joy to feel,
As GOD's love unchang'd—shall surely reveal!
When earth's silver and gold are trod into dust,
Like the sad hearts that gave them their hapless
    trust.
Turn then! ye sorrowing! the time is not past,
Oh, remember!—it may not, it cannot last!
And your hearts shall faint, that loved worship to
    yield,
When ye find the "treasure" of the heavenly field!

On the Life and Death of Flowers.

EMBLEMS are ye, of learest thoughts that o'er our
    spirits steal,
As though to us, ye would, GOD's deep, far mysteries
    reveal!
And when ye fade so fast, and pass away,
Soon wearied with your transient stay,
Ye seem like those whom we have lov'd too well,
Returning in holier climes to dwell!
Who weep, and who whisper their fond farewell!
So delicately fair! so beautiful are ye!—
Like a fond dream of love, and hope, and purity!
Ye seem like spirits from a brighter land,
Clad with sweet fragrance, and with beauty bland,
Whose life but beauty is! and death! oh sweeter
    still,
Free from the world's rude blighting touch of wrong
    and ill.
Such was Thy life of purity and love, O LORD of
    heaven;

But to Thine all holy, and "most precious death"
   was given,

For us—to gain immortal fruits of glory there,

That we, of dust, might Thy transcendent "likeness"
   bear !

Oh Saviour! God! who for the lost ones to whom
   Thou gav'st breath,

Couldest pardon purchase only, through the travail
   pangs of death !

To T . . . .

I HAVE had hopes for thee, mine own dear boy!
With blessing fraught, with more than mortal joy!
For I have felt that thou mightest be,
A chosen steward of GOD's mystery!
To tell of Him whose words and deeds of awe,
Till then, " ear never heard, eye never saw."
Oh task of sweetness,—if thou knew'st His love,
Secret of joy, all happiness above,
" He is the Bright Pathway" to the Eternal Throne,
He shall Himself to thee reveal, in thoughts un-
    known;
And He will show thee " great and mighty things,"
That whisper to trust in the love that brings
Hopes too fair for earth,
Bright with heav'nly birth!
Calling us from this vale of tears,
To share His own immortal years
That end not! There, to meet on that eternal shore,
And in " His beauty clad," unto our dear LORD pour

Our spirit's ecstacy! Ah! would'st thou know
This sweetest of hope's treasures here below,
Ask Him, in youth, to show Himself to thee!
Most true and glorious mystery!—
His promise sure!—remember! plead!
And thy spirit shall know indeed,
That dear love manifest on earth,
" His precious gift"! thy second birth!
That birth to glory, upon which sure joy,
All sorrow shall fall lightly; nor destroy
" That springing well of endless life;"
That mighty shield, through mortal strife!
'Tis happiness to bear His Cross,
And count "for Him" all things but loss!
Oh! thus "to know Him," and to feel that He is thine,
To whom all pow'r is given! for " His Blood Divine"
The dreadful ransom paid!—too dearly bought!
By His most precious sufferings wrought!
Ah! think, if He so loved thee, oh my son,
If we could understand the heav'n He hath won,
No sin, no doubt, could keep us from " His feet"!
With sorrowing love, with trust and worship meet.
" The keys of Death and Hell" are in those " Glorious
   Hands"!
E'en His—who of justice dread, hath paid the stern
   demands.

His Spirit seek! oh, seek in fondest prayer! make
 Him thy guide!
And in the shelter of His love, He shall thy spirit
 hide,
While the angels are watching that thou shalt not
 stray,
From the " narrow path" leading to endless day.
My Redeemer watch o'er thee by day and by night,
Nor suffer thy spirit to be cast from His sight.
To His arms I commit thee, in life and in death,
Who to bring thee to GOD, gave " His own divine
 breath"!
Oh ask, yea, entreat Him, to wake in thine heart,
The love that constrained Him from heaven to part,
That He might bring thee to His FATHER's throne;
And claim thee there,—all spotless, for His own!
In the joy heart knows not, in Love Divine,
Unheard, unseen, save in that Form Benign!

On Forgetfulness in Death.

Remember me, when passed away, · my lov'd, my
    left awhile,

Forget not one, whose dearest hope was to see you
    without guile,

Whose mind in earnest tenderness hung o'er your
    spirit's weal,

Still, oh still, remember me, while yours has power
    to feel!

And oh! forget not then—when on your youth the
    world shall kindly smile,

And they may seek your wavering spirits from Purity
    to wile.

And when all seem to greet you well,

Oh! bring about your hearts the spell,

My love remember still!—and when, alas! in after
    years,

Your spirits feel a loneliness, a weight too great for
    tears!

For you I've felt that sorrow, that hidden grief so
    drear,

Ah! yet remember me! while life has power to cheer,
And when your wounded spirit nears,
The brink of sad unbidden tears!
When your heart to true love cleaves,
And sorrow around it leaves
Sweet thoughts of those who sleep in peace,
Where hope, and joy, shall never cease.
Oh, then, remember me! but when God's love shall
　　on you shine,
In new born hope! in bright and secret joy! that
　　none divine!
When the thought of His deep rest,
Seems your heart's most dear request.
" Watch then and pray—" in faith and fear!
For " He who died for you" is near!

On Affection.

WHY should we seek for love on earth ?
The fragile gift of mortal birth,
While the Eternal GOD but waits to bless !
To fold in His immortal tenderness,
And turn from that Almighty love, so sweet !
The fate of griev'd and broken hearts to meet !
Ah ! did we know the joy we leave
Around our bosoms, but to weave,
While vainly waiting for a brighter morrow,
Perchance, a yet lengthening chain of sorrow !
We to that refuge should repair,
With tears to claim our dear-bought share,
And hasten with the love uncherish'd here,
To the exhaustless Fount of all most dear !
Oh, ye ! that wound the heart, that round you clings,
'Tis thus ye lend to it a spirit's wings !—
And through that grief, so strangely sad,—so darkly
    drear,
First bid us to our long-forsaken GOD draw near !

G

In His dear love to rest! where change is not, nor
  pain,
Nor aught of ill shall the lone spirit know again!
And when at last, around your hearts regret shall
  fall,
And thoughts of that forsaken love, your minds
  appal!
Oh! in that dark hour!—so sad, so lone!
Turn to the " Great Soother!" still thine own!
And the world forsaking,
To His dear love waking!—
Give to Him the spirit that earth so mars,
Born for a brighter home, beyond the stars!
Where CHRIST, our LORD! shall give thee back once
  more
In heaven, thy loved, and long lost store!

To R . . .

WHEN thou shalt walk amid the waves of life,
And take thy part in that unequal strife,
If thou should'st taste the bitter tears of ill,
In the heart's depths! which GOD alone can fill!
Or shouldest thou, mid ev'ry joy, still feel alone,
While all thy fairest hopes shall lose their false
    bright tone;
Ah! then, bethink thee in that solemn hour,
Of Him who holds thee in His viewless pow'r,
Of that invisible! mysterious guide!
The "Holy One"! Who on the Cross hath died!
Of Him who whispers to thy soul, when none of
    earth are near,
Though angels haply glide around thee, those dear
    sounds to hear.
Oh! yes—loved as thou hast been through long, long
    years,
Thou must go forth alone, along the vale of tears!
Yet, not alone!—and when thou too shalt grief's sad
    secrets know,

And wander on in loneliness! in darkness here
   below!
There is an Eye that fondly marks those tears;
And waits and watches till thy pray'r He hears!
When "that small still voice," that whisper—bids
   thee pray,
'Tis the voice of thy GOD! oh! turn not away!
But "call upon Him then"—in prayer so deep,
That thy spirit shall cast off her deathly sleep.
And thou shalt know joy, that shall to thee seem,
Like the blessed thoughts of an angel's dream!
Oh! bright are those moments of GOD's dear love,
Sent down in their mystery, from above!—
Like "the wind that bloweth from on high,"
Through the far realms of the boundless sky;
"Whence it cometh we know not, nor whither it
   goes"!
Like the deep fond secret of the spirit's repose!
Such be thy portion, too blest to tell;
"The Peace of GOD" in thine heart's lone cell,
That measureless joy, thou shalt yet surely find,
If thou seek it—with a true and loving mind!
For He calls thee forth to walk in His light,
In the narrow path love hath made so bright!
And leave to the world its sickly treasure,
For joy unspeakable! without measure!—

Yes ! watch for the " Holy Bridegroom's cry" !
Feel, and believe Him for ever nigh!
For He cometh—He cometh to the soul on earth,
That sweet, secret messenger of Divinest birth !
And shall make thy spirit too deeply blest,
Unearthly type of her heavenly rest !

On Unkindness.

Oh ! think what 'tis ye do ! who cast love's gift
 away
In carelessness, or scorn to seek another stay.
Here, joy hath no full measure,
Save in the heart's fond treasure.
Oh ! think what 'tis ye do ! then prize it while 'tis
 lent,
That happy dream !—that brief bright light in pity
 sent,
That surest foretaste of full joy, that here to us is
 given :
Lest it ne'er again should bloom for you on this dark
 side of heav'n :
It may not even visit you till in long after years,—
It sweeps the chord of memory in anguish and in
 tears !—
Oh ! watch it ! and still garner in, love's dearest,
 fondest smile,
Ere it fade and flee away, like a spirit without guile.

Then, shall it unite with the Seraphim!
That reflection from the rays of Him,
To whom alone all glory is but dim!—
In Whose dread, Whose uncreated light,
The radiant heavens are not bright!
" The Faithful and the True," who sendeth from
  the sky,
Those voices sweet! those blessed tokens ever nigh!
All such love—be sure, is borrowed from on High!
Oh think, if in wrath God took it hence, in Paradise
  to bloom,
And left thee sad and desolate, to thy soul's de-
  sponding gloom.
Think! if the heart that lov'd thee well—in the grave
  should shrouded lie,
And thou wert left to wander here, in thy lonely
  misery!

On Sleep.

When " Thy Bright Eye" has bound me,
When Thine angels surround me,
And my spirit to rest is given—
Hear then, my God—oh hear !—from heaven !
And send Thy messengers of love,
With sweetest tokens from above,
That I, too, may, ere I wake,
Of Thine holiness partake !
For to the soul, indeed, forgiven ;
Sleep's tender boon, in love, is given
As a pledge of her rest in heaven !
And when we sink in that deep trance,—
It seems all pure things to enhance !
And in that gentle seeming
To wear a spirit's meaning.
Oh ! I have seen mysterious things in sleep,
With thoughts unknown, unutterably sweet,
As though an angel's hand had lift the veil,
Bidding us, lovingly, our Saviour hail—

" And look (in awe) on Him"! at length,
The glory of Whose Face shall be,
Begirt with His Infinity,
" As the sun shining in his strength"!
From the glory of " That Face,"
Brightening eternal space,
" The heavens, and earth shall flee away;"
" Nor shall place be found for them," nor stay,
In the Judgment's dread and wrathful day.
Ah! when we wake from death's long night,
Oh! who shall hide us, in Thy sight?·
When at that Great Eternal Bar we stand,
'Tis Thou alone canst hold us in Thine hand!
To Thee! to Thee! oh nothing can we bring,
Yet still to Thee, alone—our spirits cling.
"Stricken" for us—"oh Lamb of God"!—wert Thou!
" Bruised and wounded" was that " Blessed Brow,"
On whom the angels dare not gaze,
Save in still wonder and amaze!
And eyes they veil—(to look on Him)
The bright, the blazing, Seraphim!
Not angel tongue could tell the joy with Thee to be!
Who by Thine own!—Thy priceless ransom set us
    free!
Oh! sweet to die,—so we for ever wake with Thee!

On Repentance.

RETURN, poor wanderer! return, repent,
The night is at hand, the day's far spent:
Return!—the tender FATHER waits for thee,
His own, His ransom'd from eternity!
New worlds within His Smile shall open to thine eyes,
And things, that yet "thou know'st not," o'er thy
    spirit rise!
Oh then, tempt not "the wrath of GOD"!—nor tarry
    till too late,
Till e'en the angel of His love, forbidden is to wait!
For there are tears the heart must weep,—
While lowly thoughts will sadly sweep
O'er our bosom's sorrow; yet, oh shun not that
    grief, that fear;
So shall thy woe be changed—to joy so bright, to
    hopes most dear!—
Oh! yes, believe it, though the soul be riv'n,
Where GOD's Spirit not in vain hath striven,
In dread and gracious power!
LORD! give us but that sacred hour!

That we unto Thy mighty strength may cling,
And hide us in the shelter of Thy wing!
Passing into the shadow of Thy bitter Cross,
Oh! only there!—to feel our brightest joys "but loss."
Alas! and is it from Thine awful woe,
(For us so gently suffer'd here below;)
Our wells of everlasting gladness spring;
And cam'st Thou down in vain on love's sweet wing, ⎫
To taste the bitterest cup of death's keen sting, ⎬
Yet we still turn from Thy dread Agony ⎭
To earth!—to withering hopes, and vanity!

On Happiness.

BRIGHT sweet vision of our youth, though type of
    heav'n alone !—

That glorious, unearthly light, from off the eternal
    Throne !

The foretaste and sure pledge—of joy, that GOD shall
    give

To those who in His sight alone desire to live !

Here,—it cannot last for ever, how fair so e'er
    it be ;

Oh ! then, in its hopes, oh never—let thine heart
    garner'd be !

It was Love Eternal gave it, it was love "that took
    away,"

To show thee " great and mighty things" in the dark
    and stormy day, ·

It shall be found hereafter; if, indeed, thou shalt
    faithful prove,

To thine own, thy gracious Master,—whose " Holy
    Name" is Love !

But here we idols make ! foundations lay,

Where the " rust and moth corrupt" in sure
   decay,

Withering to dust, alas ! our brightest day !

There are, amid those griev'd hearts, who 'neath life's
   shadows feel

Such woe—shall yet to them a mightier love reveal !

They know what 'twas—that rent " That ever blessed
   Brow" !

To Whom the hosts of heav'n shall never cease to bow.

Our sin transfix'd " those loving hands," which " the
   clouds in light array'd !"

At whose dread touch—the mighty waves, the wildest
   winds were stayed !—

" It pleas'd the FATHER that in Him all fulness
   should for ever dwell !"

" All things should bow" in heav'n and earth, and in
   the darkest depths of hell !

But we forsake His promise sure,

To find too late, nought may endure ;

For all shall be as darkness, where GOD is not.

As the still undying worm—that fatal lot—

'Tis He alone can still the yearnings of the heart,

And to the fallen soul " eternal life impart."

Ah ! could'st thou trust thy fond hopes here,

All—thou hast felt so true ! so dear

H

To the bosom of thy " redeeming GOD" commit that
   care,

That thou and thine, in joy eternal may'st for ever
   share.

Sweet the foretaste—sweeter shall the fulness be,

When " clothed with His own Immortality !"

" Thy LORD shall lead thee" to that fountain running
   o'er

Of joy eternal !—and of love's exhaustless store !

To an Infant named Theodora.

My last, my lov'd, my little one, to me,
Thy young, and gentle spirit seem'd to be,
Like one from sin and woe for ever free,
As though thou wert a messenger of love,
Sent down from out God's Paradise above!
To whisper to my lonely heart of joys beyond the
  tomb,
Where brightest things shall meet no more with
  Death's untimely doom!—
Sweet child of dearest hopes—in after years!
Live not for this dim world's sad hopes and fears,
This valley dark! of solitary tears,
But live to Him!—for Him!—"who died for thee,"
And of His dread Holiness, partaker be!
So shalt thou return unto His lov'd embrace,
Pure and unsullied, from thine earthly race,
To those transcendent joys, at "God's right hand!"
Where thou'lt be found amid the heavenly band.
Truly (a gift) from heaven wert thou,
Giv'n to heal my broken spirit now,

And soothe the tears, that e'er must fall,
Till the heart thrills at Death's dread call!—
Ah!—when in thy sweet lineaments I trace,
Unearthly calmness, in that fair young face!
Oh! then, thou seem'st as one, but lent to earth,
A tender blossom of a holier birth!—
In thy young beauty, a deep mystery lies,
Telling of thy bright, far home, beyond the skies!
Where thou, my darling, on thy SAVIOUR's breast
Shalt lay thy weeping heart!—and be at rest!

On Conscience.

Oh hearken ! for 'tis faint and low,
Softer, than sweetest sound below!
That " still small voice " !—Though all unheard
Of earth—that more than angel's word,
Messenger of love, minister of God—ah ! if slighted,
Who shall tell how far, alas ! the soul, when thus
    benighted,
Shall fall away ? Was it for this, Thou, Lord,
    did'st die ?
For this, Thy lonely woe ! Thy nameless "agony"!
That we should pass " Thy secret counsel" lightly
    by ?
Oh ! rather bid us " hide our face and bow,"
Like the Great Seer of Horeb ! even now,
It strives within us !—dreadful whisper ! warning
    kind—
Oh constrain our hearts to listen !—touch Thou the
    mind
Of wilful sin ; make us to feel Thy pow'r,
In that of " everlasting love" ! Thine hour

To know, O Lord! Thou hast been near,
And bade our worldly spirits, hear!
"Leave us not," oh! leave us not in hate,
Unto the just, the dread earned fate,
Of those that "strive with God!"—for 'tis Thine
To show us, in that "still voice" divine,
Unearthly hope!—beyond the reach of tears,
The wasted promise of our bygone years.
'Tis thus that "God the soul allureth" with a
  brighter love,
Sure token of her great heritage!—her sweet home
  above.
On sin of heart, or thought—such dare not look ;
Nor to obtain earth's dearest—could they brook,
The o'ershadowing of "that gracious Brow,"
Whose tender presence is their heaven now!
Oh! then, "quench not" "that voice," on which the
  angels live !—
Whose love remaineth !—even God no more could
  give !

On the Blessedness of Death.

"Blessed are the dead, that die in the Lord," ah! yet,
Not dead, as we call death!—oh, think it not, nor let
The faithless hope it, they wait "the Bridegroom's
   voice"—they sleep in Him!
Ah!—who shall tell the rapture of that, "His rest,"
   no change can dim!
Henceforth, mightily, unto God they live, their new
   born life
Shall close no more!—passed are sin's dark waters,
   and the strife
Of earth! the spirits God made free,—
Dear purchase of His agony,—
In regions all too bright, for evermore are past
Into that joy! that with Eternity shall last!
Then ask not thy loved ones from on high,
To life's long tears, and griefs passed by;
Stay not their spirit's joyous wing,
Nor to their changeless glory bring,
One sad and earthly token!
They rest in hope unbroken!—
No! wish not thy dear ones thence,
In "eternal peace" from hence

God's love is still enfolding,
The weary ones upholding.
The Redeemer now is near,
To the hearts that pain wrung here,
And there in bliss reclining,
Where God's Great Glory's shining,
The bright ones rest!—ah! yes, their spirits pass'd away,
Or e'er the shadows fell—the dearest hopes betray.
Life's deepest woe they knew not—they shall never know
When the lone heart breaks on in darkness here below.
When the soul widow'd cries to God in pain,
With vain regrets, ne'er to be heal'd again.
Nevertheless, the soul on Thee, my God, shall live e'en then,
Her "portion infinite! her guide to glory"! and when
Her "heart and flesh shall fail," O Christ, draw near!
With " Words Divine," the soul alone can hear !
Mid night's dark shadows, still our spirits bear !
Ah then ! oh baffled Death ! thou art not there !
Thus ! thus ! once more !—God's precious life is pour'd,
Yea, " blessed are the dead, that die in the Lord!"

Gloria in excelsis Deo.

JOSEPH MASTERS AND CO., PRINTERS, ALDERSGATE STREET.